This book belongs to:

Name _____

Email _____

Phone _____

If found, please: ○ Read ○ Use ○ Return ○ Sell ○ Burn

Self-portrait (drawn with eyes closed)

It is what it is.

I am here now

A creative mindfulness
guide and journal

The
Mindfulness
Project

EBURY
PRESS

Table of contents

Table of exercises

(p.4) Circle the page numbers of exercises you want to do.

(p.4) Strike through if partially completed.

(p.4) Cross out when complete.

Hello reader

Whether you are new to mindfulness or an experienced meditator, there is so much to discover in each moment. This book contains cues and tools to help you approach your moment-to-moment experience with a renewed sense of curiosity – and document it with creativity. Make this your field guide as you set out to explore life through the lens of mindfulness.

With practice, you may begin to see your internal experiences and the world around you in a new way – maybe noticing things and recognizing patterns that you hadn't before. Be curious and brave as you turn your attention to all the things you encounter – the good, the bad and the ugly. Let it all inspire and intrigue you. By cultivating certain qualities along the way, even the smallest discoveries can hold huge potential to enrich our lives with more insight, joy and new meaning.

The exercises that lie ahead range from the slightly absurd to the tear jerking and soul searching. To get the most out of them, we also encourage you to practise mindfulness through meditation (you can access a guided meditation by Tara Brach on our website) and use the space at the back for your notes.

Go for it: fill the pages of this book with your journey – be honest, be kind and be here now!

:) The Mindfulness Project

How to use this book

There are two main ways to practise mindfulness: formally, through meditation, and informally, by bringing it into our everyday lives. This field guide is designed to support you in both. It includes instructions for meditating, as well as a wide range of other exercises that will help make mindfulness relevant and meaningful in your daily life.

Here are some suggestions on how to use it:

1. The introduction section includes some tips and ground rules.

2. In particular, keep the 'Frames of mindfulness' on page 12 in mind while doing the exercises.

3. Exercises don't need to be completed in any order.

4. Use the 'Table of exercises' on page vii to navigate.

5. Adapt and make the exercises relevant for you.

6. Skip things, do things more than once, assign exercises to others.

7. Meditate using the guided audio outlined on page 18 and available on our website.

8. Use the 'Meditation field notes' pages in the back (from page 167) for your notes.

Use this book and mindfulness to explore your inherent creativity and the inspiration of each moment in a playful, curious and non-judgemental way. All of these pages are for you to document your discoveries in whatever creative way you feel inspired to. There are no right or wrong answers and there is no one way to express yourself.

Here are some ideas we've had:

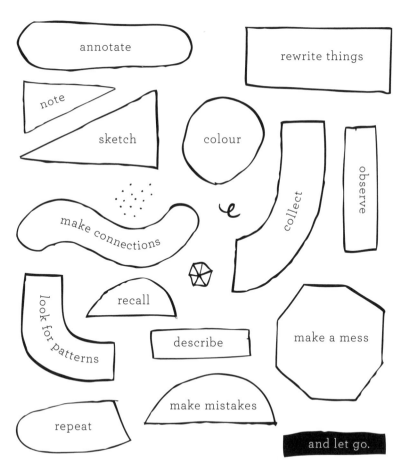

annotate

rewrite things

note

sketch

colour

observe

make connections

collect

look for patterns

recall

describe

make a mess

make mistakes

repeat

and let go.

Definitions of mindfulness

Our definition:

Mindfulness is a simple and very powerful practice of training our attention. It's simple in that it's really just about paying attention to what's happening here and now (i.e. sensations, thoughts and emotions) in a non-judgemental way. It's powerful because it can interrupt the habit of getting lost in thoughts, mostly about the future or past, which often generates more stress on top of the real pressures of everyday life.

Someone else's definition:

'Mindfulness is simply being aware of what is happening right now without wishing it were different; enjoying the pleasant without holding on when it changes (which it will); being with the unpleasant without fearing it will always be this way (which it won't).'

James Baraz

Your definition:

Now or later.

An illustration?

Some words?

_____

_____

_____

_____

_____

_____

_____

_____

_____

_____

_____

Search for meaning...

G	Z	M	L	R	A	C	C	E	P	T	A	N	C	E
Q	C	R	E	A	T	I	V	I	T	Y	E	Z	D	F
B	V	P	R	E	S	E	N	C	E	D	Z	B	D	K
I	A	N	R	T	M	F	E	K	T	Y	C	Z	Q	E
K	A	O	J	C	Y	E	Y	N	Q	K	O	D	O	R
M	C	Y	U	O	E	E	D	W	Y	U	N	P	F	W
U	M	U	X	M	E	L	O	I	Y	V	N	G	J	M
A	E	J	R	P	C	V	R	J	T	A	E	P	V	H
F	L	L	S	A	N	I	T	Y	M	A	C	P	G	C
S	T	R	E	S	S	R	E	D	U	C	T	I	O	N
L	S	E	N	S	O	R	Y	R	Z	B	I	I	X	J
T	X	Q	K	I	X	X	A	O	I	N	O	B	O	Y
A	F	M	R	O	Q	I	I	G	P	K	N	W	U	N
X	Z	O	R	N	X	Z	F	G	Q	D	T	M	I	G
J	N	O	N	J	U	D	G	E	M	E	N	T	A	L

There are 10 key words to discover. How many can you find?

(Other winning words not found in the wordsearch)

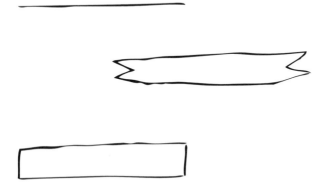

Timeline of modern mindfulness

Instructions: Circle the things that you've come across.

Add: Personal retreats. When you first meditated. Discovered your favourite meditation teachers/places. Other books read. Challenges/Milestones. Soul-searching journeys. Your birthday.

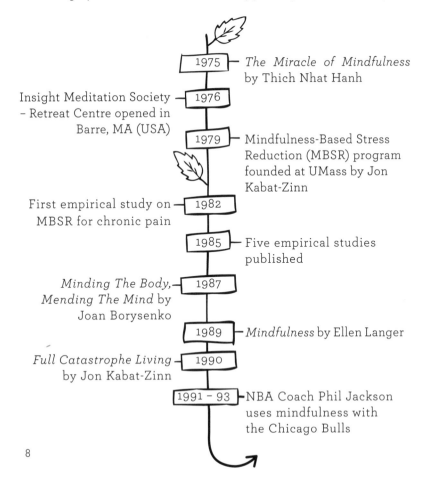

1975 — *The Miracle of Mindfulness* by Thich Nhat Hanh

Insight Meditation Society – Retreat Centre opened in Barre, MA (USA) — **1976**

1979 — Mindfulness-Based Stress Reduction (MBSR) program founded at UMass by Jon Kabat-Zinn

First empirical study on MBSR for chronic pain — **1982**

1985 — Five empirical studies published

Minding The Body, Mending The Mind by Joan Borysenko — **1987**

1989 — *Mindfulness* by Ellen Langer

Full Catastrophe Living by Jon Kabat-Zinn — **1990**

1991 – 93 — NBA Coach Phil Jackson uses mindfulness with the Chicago Bulls

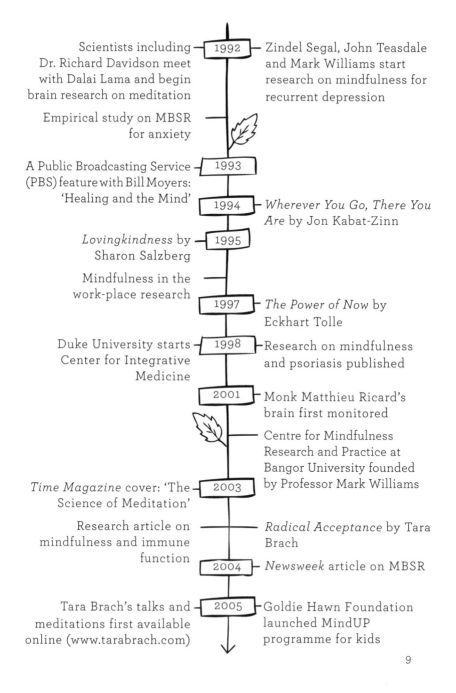

Scientists including Dr. Richard Davidson meet with Dalai Lama and begin brain research on meditation

1992 — Zindel Segal, John Teasdale and Mark Williams start research on mindfulness for recurrent depression

Empirical study on MBSR for anxiety

A Public Broadcasting Service (PBS) feature with Bill Moyers: 'Healing and the Mind' — **1993**

1994 — *Wherever You Go, There You Are* by Jon Kabat-Zinn

Lovingkindness by Sharon Salzberg — **1995**

Mindfulness in the work-place research

1997 — *The Power of Now* by Eckhart Tolle

Duke University starts Center for Integrative Medicine — **1998** — Research on mindfulness and psoriasis published

2001 — Monk Matthieu Ricard's brain first monitored

Centre for Mindfulness Research and Practice at Bangor University founded by Professor Mark Williams

Time Magazine cover: 'The Science of Meditation' — **2003**

Research article on mindfulness and immune function — *Radical Acceptance* by Tara Brach

2004 — *Newsweek* article on MBSR

Tara Brach's talks and meditations first available online (www.tarabrach.com) — **2005** — Goldie Hawn Foundation launched MindUP programme for kids

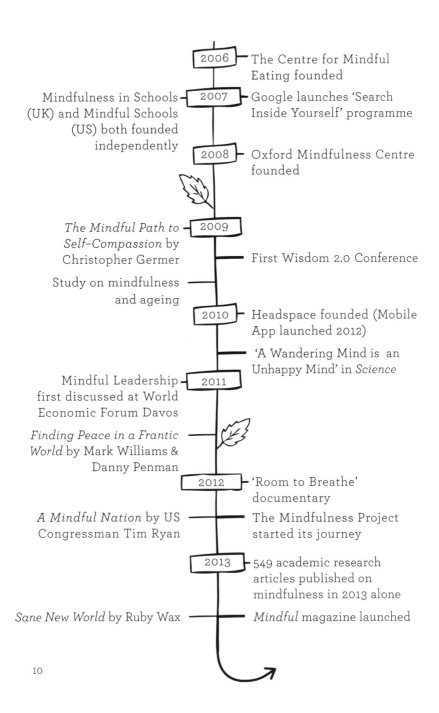

2006 — The Centre for Mindful Eating founded

Mindfulness in Schools (UK) and Mindful Schools (US) both founded independently — **2007** — Google launches 'Search Inside Yourself' programme

2008 — Oxford Mindfulness Centre founded

The Mindful Path to Self-Compassion by Christopher Germer — **2009**

First Wisdom 2.0 Conference

Study on mindfulness and ageing

2010 — Headspace founded (Mobile App launched 2012)

'A Wandering Mind is an Unhappy Mind' in *Science*

Mindful Leadership first discussed at World Economic Forum Davos — **2011**

Finding Peace in a Frantic World by Mark Williams & Danny Penman

2012 — 'Room to Breathe' documentary

A Mindful Nation by US Congressman Tim Ryan — The Mindfulness Project started its journey

2013 — 549 academic research articles published on mindfulness in 2013 alone

Sane New World by Ruby Wax — *Mindful* magazine launched

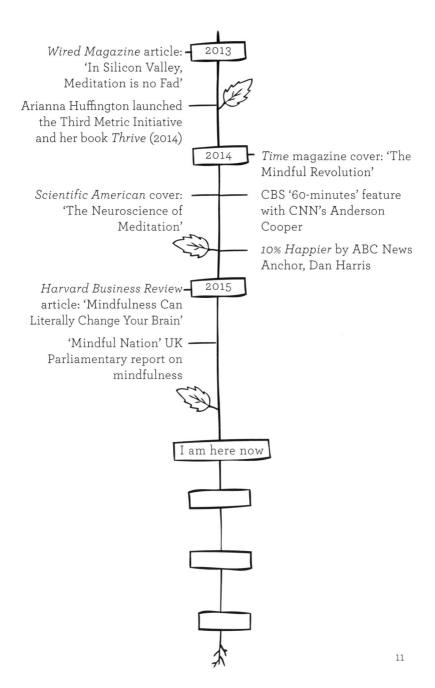

Wired Magazine article: '2013'
'In Silicon Valley,
Meditation is no Fad'

Arianna Huffington launched
the Third Metric Initiative
and her book *Thrive* (2014)

2014 — *Time* magazine cover: 'The
Mindful Revolution'

Scientific American cover:
'The Neuroscience of
Meditation'

CBS '60-minutes' feature
with CNN's Anderson
Cooper

10% Happier by ABC News
Anchor, Dan Harris

Harvard Business Review 2015
article: 'Mindfulness Can
Literally Change Your Brain'

'Mindful Nation' UK
Parliamentary report on
mindfulness

I am here now

Frames of mindfulness – the ground rules

These are the ground rules for practising mindfulness, both in using this book and beyond. They are attitudes or frames of mind that help cut through some of the challenges that keep us from being fully present in our lives. Bookmark this page and return here often. *

1. Here now
Anytime you're swept away in thoughts about the past or future, notice that your mind has drifted off and gently bring your attention back to the present moment – by focusing on an anchor such as your breath, a specific part of your body or sounds.

2. Non-judging
Practise paying attention to your thoughts and the judgements your mind tends to make. Don't try to stop or resist them, just curiously notice them. The mind is like a label maker.

3. Patience
Have patience with the way your experience with mindfulness unfolds. Also have patience with each moment, even when it's uncomfortable and your mind would rather rush to the next. Be patient with the wandering nature of your mind. Treat it as you would a puppy being trained to sit.

4. Be kind to yourself
Be gentle and treat yourself with kindness. Mindfulness allows us to recognize and turn towards some painful thoughts and emotions. In those moments, it can help to adopt an attitude of compassion toward ourselves – just like you would turn with warmth and kindness to a friend who might be having a rough time.

5. Beginner's mind

Sometimes the mind likes to think it has seen all there is to see or that it knows all it needs to know. Let's call it the 'Know-It-All-Mind'. Try returning to every exercise and practice, and even each moment, with a new sense of curiosity and stay open to discovery. That's when real surprises and magic happen.

6. Trust

Trust your own basic wisdom and intuition. This doesn't mean always trusting your thoughts. Mindfulness will help you see that those come, go, and change.

7. Non-striving

Sometimes we come to mindfulness hoping to solve our problems or change and improve ourselves. But this sense of wanting things to be different can be an obstacle to truly experiencing mindfulness. The practice of mindfulness is not about being somewhere else or different, but rather just being with and accepting what's here now.

8. Acceptance

Accept that things are the way they are in each moment. That doesn't mean they won't change or can't be changed.
Pain x Resistance = Suffering
Pain = Pain

9. Letting go

Practise letting go of clinging to ideas, thoughts, control, or wanting things to be a certain way. Notice what it feels like in your body when you're clinging vs. letting go.

10. Commitment

Mindfulness is a practice, but it's not just meditation. We can take mindfulness into all aspects of our lives. Make a commitment to both meditating and practising mindfulness as a way of living/being.

*These are adapted from *Full Catastrophe Living* by Jon Kabat-Zinn

13

Mindfulness quiz

For each statement below, enter the number from the scale that best corresponds to how often you experience these things.

1 Never	2 Rarely	3 Sometimes	4 Frequently	5 Always

1.	When I'm walking somewhere and pass a flower along the way, I stop to smell it.	
2.	I tend to worry about the future and/or regret things from the past.	
3.	Take time to really savour my food.	
4.	Race from one place to the next without noticing what's along the way.	
5.	Get caught up in my own thoughts while someone else is speaking.	
6.	Notice what happens in my body, when I'm stressed (e.g. fast heart beat, muscle tension)	
7.	Can be comfortable just sitting and watching a sunset.	
8.	After an argument I carry on thinking of all the things I could have said to prove my point.	
9.	Am lost in thought when I could be enjoying a sensory experience, like a kiss.	

10. Get impatient while waiting in a queue, at a red light or for public transport.	
11. Take time to pause and feel grateful for the things I have going for me.	
12. Am hard on myself when I've made a mistake.	
13. Often try to 'think myself out' of problems and situations.	
14. Pay attention to sounds, like wind blowing through the trees, cars passing by, or rain falling.	
Sum of answers to questions 1, 3, 6, 7, 11, 14 =	
ADD 34 =	
SUBTRACT the sum of answers to questions 2, 4, 5, 8, 9, 10, 12, 13 =	
Total Score =	

Score

0 – 18: Beginner. You may find yourself frequently lost in thought and missing out on the present moment. Keep practising.

19 – 38: Pretty mindful. You may have regular mindful moments, when you are being present with whatever you encounter. Keep practising.

39 – 56: Almost enlightened. Keep practising.

How to be here now

'Mindfulness means paying attention in a particular way: on purpose, in the present moment, and nonjudgementally.'

Jon Kabat-Zinn

I am here now...

...when I tune into my <u>senses</u> and what I'm feeling in my body right this moment.

...when I <u>observe</u> and <u>investigate</u> my inner world at this moment, without being harsh or judgemental.

...when I <u>concentrate</u> my attention on a specific present-moment experience, such as my breath.

...when I pay attention to and <u>cultivate</u> the good things in my life and the warm-and-fuzzy feelings they give me.

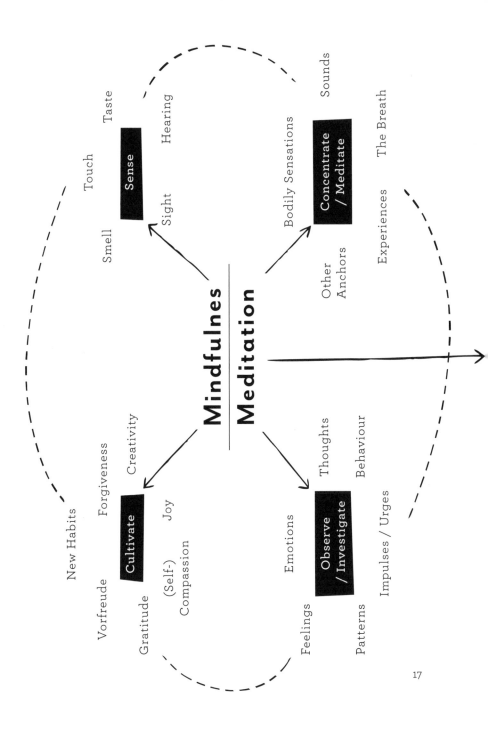

Mindfulnes Meditation

Sense
- Taste
- Hearing
- Touch
- Sight
- Smell

Concentrate / Meditate
- Sounds
- Bodily Sensations
- The Breath
- Other Anchors
- Experiences

Cultivate
- Creativity
- Forgiveness
- Joy
- Vorfreude
- (Self-) Compassion
- Gratitude

Observe / Investigate
- Thoughts
- Behaviour
- Emotions
- Impulses / Urges
- Feelings
- Patterns

New Habits

Meditation

Meditation helps us build the 'mindfulness muscle' of our minds, so that we can have more mindful moments throughout our days and build resilience to all we encounter in our lives.

You'll find a 25-minute guided meditation by Tara Brach at:

iamherenow.com

The audio file is broken up into the following sections. Follow the instructions given. This can be done sitting down, standing up or lying flat. See page 168 for 'Tips on how to sit'.

Start slowly, but daily. Build up your practice over time. Keep the Frames of mindfulness (page 12) in mind.

0–5 mins	Arriving in the body
5–10 mins	Mindfulness of the breath
10–15 mins	Mindfulness of sounds
15–25 mins	Open awareness of body, breath, sounds & thoughts

Document your findings in the field notes pages located at the back of this book.

10 ways to make your day more mindful...

Cut or tear out this page, stick it on the wall, put it in your wallet, take a photo, share it.

1. Meditate, even if it's just for a few minutes.
2. Slow down and tune into your body and senses.
3. Don't argue with reality – it is what it is.
4. Pay attention to people, especially your loved ones.
5. Think of one thing you're grateful for before going to bed.
6. Go easy on and be kind to yourself, even when you blow it.
7. When good things happen, pause and notice how it feels.
8. When not so good things happen, pause. Notice how it feels.
9. Upon stressing out, take three deep breaths.
10. Connect at least once a day with nature.

Exercises

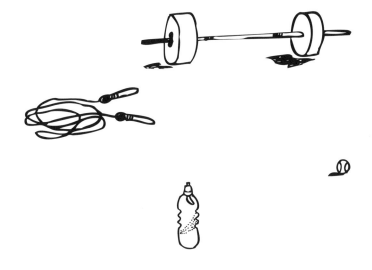

Present penny

Put a penny in the middle of the book...
in the **NOW.**

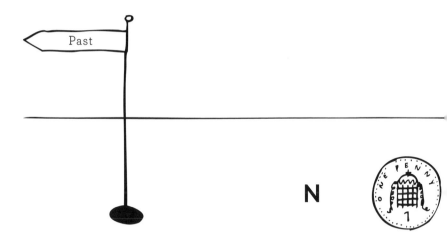

Then try to put the penny in the **PAST...**
or in the **FUTURE.**

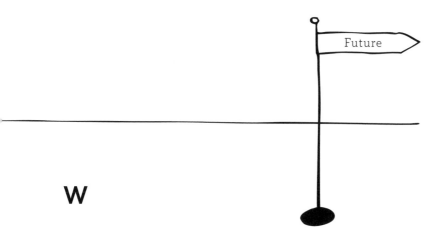

W

Future

Solution: No matter where you place the penny, it's still in the now.

23

Anchor, man

Keep your attention focused on the intersection of the X for one minute (set your alarm).

When your mind w a n d e r s, just gently bring your attention back.

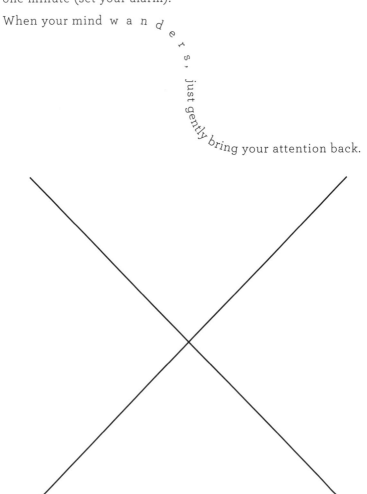

Examples

Set your sights on other visual anchors out there. Draw
the possibilities here and use this page as a reminder.

Vital signs – breathing

Take several normal breaths in and out. Notice where you feel
your breath (check all that apply):

☐ Chest   ☐ Nose

☐ Belly   ☐ Mouth

☐ Ribcage   ☐ Throat

☐ Other _____

Where is it if you change the length of your breath? (draw arrow)

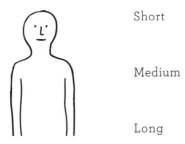

Short

Medium

Long

⚠ Often, when we are tense, our breath is in our upper chest.

Paying attention to the breath is a way of anchoring ourselves in this present moment. It is always here for us to return to if our attention drifts off to the future or past.

Daily variety

Complete this list of ways you could change your daily routine:

- wear your watch on the other wrist
- take a different path to work
- eat lunch at a different time
- brush your teeth with the opposite hand
- read a different newspaper
- sleep on the opposite side of the bed
-
-
-
-
-
-

Choose one. Try it.

'The little things? The little moments? They aren't little.'

Jon Kabat-Zinn

Gratitude a to z

A _____ Spell out the things you're grateful for.

_____ Let the letters inspire you...

B

C

D

E

F

G

H

I

J

K

L

See!

These are virtually identical patterns. Look carefully to see the differences.

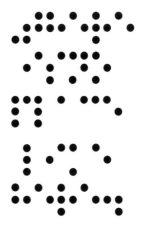

Notice the thoughts or feelings that come up.

O Boredom   O Impatience   O Anger   O Enjoyment
O Fear of overlooking something   O Other _____

_____

_____

Notes:

_____

_____

_____

_____

Extra credit: These are Braille letters. Decipher the messages.

33

Clouded thoughts

Thoughts come and go across our minds like clouds in the sky. Some bigger than others, some wispy, others round, some oval. Maybe a rain cloud...

Draw more clouds of your own and write down your thoughts. Watch them come and go against the blue sky of your mind.

TURTLE GETS WHEELS TO REPLACE INJURED LEGS!

91 YEAR OLD WOMAN BREAKS MARATHON RECORD!

Good news!

Compile positive news headlines here. Clip them out and glue them here or copy them down in your favourite colours.

Share the good news with others!

Ice cube meditation

Hold an ice cube in your hand for as long as it takes for it to melt. Let the melted ice just drop on your lap, the table, or on to these pages. Observe the sensations, uncomfortable feelings, thoughts and emotions as they arise. Record them here when you've finished.

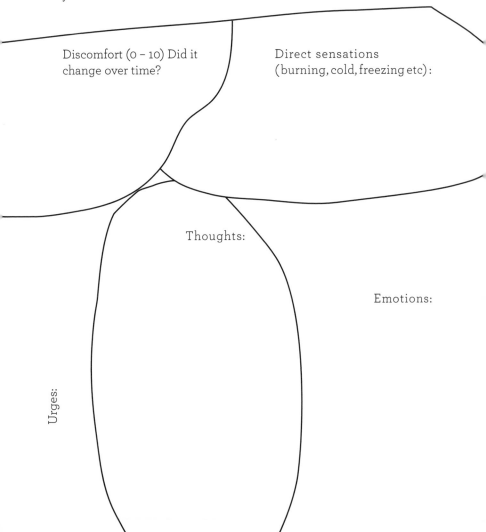

Discomfort (0 – 10) Did it change over time?

Direct sensations (burning, cold, freezing etc):

Thoughts:

Emotions:

Urges:

Cut out this page. Colour it in and use it as a bookmark for this or any other book.

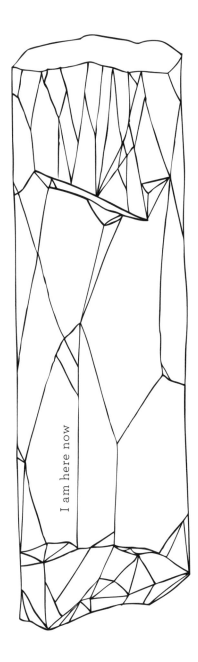

I am here now

'In this choiceless never-ending flow of life, there is an infinite array of choices. One alone brings happiness: to love what is.'

Dorothy Hunt

Counting your way home

Count the things you encounter on your way home.

Here are some ideas to try one at a time:

Number:

———   Dogs or cats you see

———   Cars driving passed you as you walk

———   Trees along the way

———   Cracks in the pavement

———   Steps you take

———   People on your train or bus

———

———

———

———

———

———

'Look with all your eyes, look.'
Jules Verne, Michael Strogoff

Connect the dots

Slowly connect the dots by number.
One line with each breath.

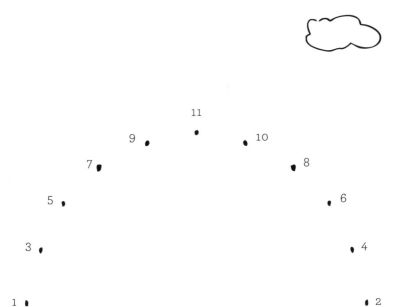

'Only that day dawns to which we are awake.'
Henry David Thoreau

The hand meditation

Trace your left hand here.

Put both hands in their place on the pages. Close your eyes. Feel the sensation of your skin on the pages. The resistance of the book, wanting to close. Feel the rhythm of your pulse or the tingling of your finger-tips?

Trace your right hand here.

Repeat as desired.

Ocean of emotion

'Our thoughts are the winds and our emotions the waters...The average length of an emotion left to its own devices is 1.5 minutes. What keeps it going beyond that?...the winds of thought.'

Tara Brach

Note the thoughts you have that stir up the waves of emotion for you.

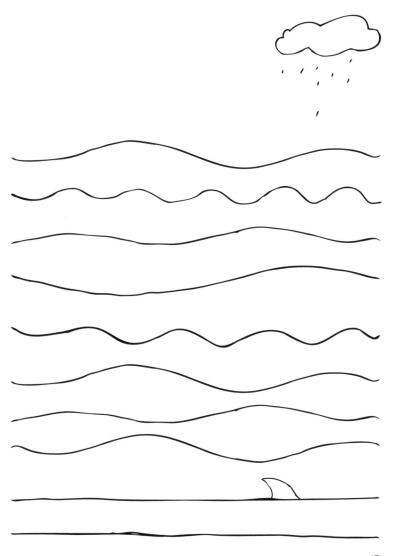

Finding your niche

Imagine all the things you need to create the perfect place to meditate in your home.

Make a plan ⟶ Make a list ⟶ Make it happen!

Ideas
Potential locations: living room, corner of bedroom...
Comfort: cushion, chair, blanket, pillow, rug, mat...
Tools: timer, bells, notebook...
Inspiration: plant, rock, vase, candles...

Notes:

_____

_____

_____

_____

_____

_____

_____

_____

Sketch:

P.S. Don't wait for the perfect conditions to meditate.

Surround sound

Listen to the sounds around you for three minutes. Be like a
microphone, just absorbing the sounds and their vibrations.
Note the things you hear and the directions they come from.

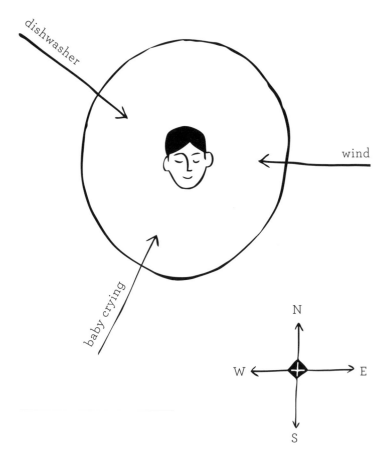

Do this at different locations
(e.g. at home or at work, on
public transport, in a park, at the
supermarket, in an aeroplane or
the dentist's office…)

Keep breathing

With each breath
in and out,
draw a line in a different direction without lifting the pen from the paper.

 Notice when your breathing gets restricted. Let your pen follow the breath rather than trying to make your breath follow the pen.

→ Repeat often, using a different coloured pen each time. Make it a modern art masterpiece by colouring in the spaces in between.

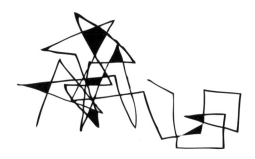

Notes:

_____

_____

_____

_____

Yours

1	Sign your name 10 times as you would normally do:

2	Sign your name 10 times but change something about it each time:

truly,

3	Sign your name again, 10 times, as normal:

Notice:

1. Notice in the first column how you're automatically able to replicate your signature.

2. See if it requires more attention to create a different version of your signature each time.

3. Are the first signatures in this column different to usual? Interrupting the auto-pilot mode even just for a short period can change our patterns.

Adapted from Pavel Somov, *Present Perfect* (2010)

Page of rage

aggressive scribble box

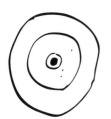

pencil-stab
point

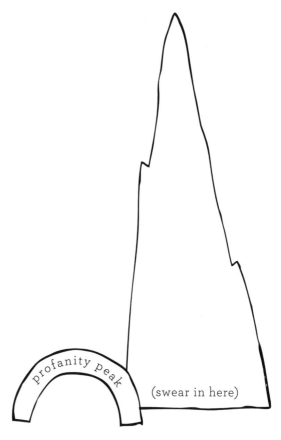

profanity peak

(swear in here)

Anti-ageing meditation

Close your eyes, focus your attention on the area around your eyes, tune into the muscles in your jaw, around your mouth, and on your forehead. Notice any tension as you take several deep breaths in. Release the tension as you breathe out.

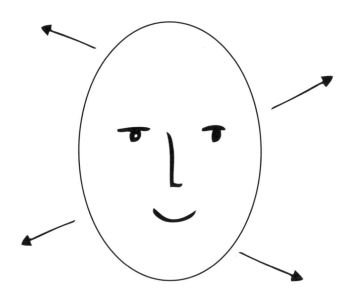

Practise three times daily for best results!

Next time you're feeling _____ , make a note of where that emotion leaves tension in your face.

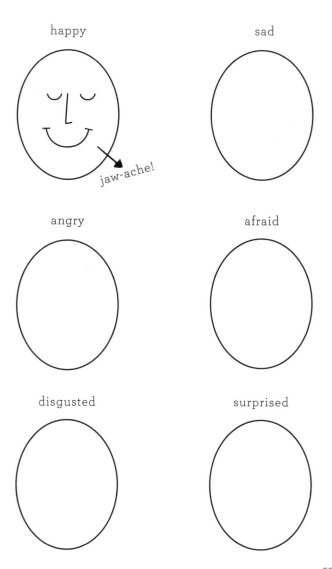

happy

sad

angry

afraid

disgusted

surprised

jaw-ache!

Fun-genda

Vor·freu·de (for-froi-duh) *noun*: the German word for the anticipatory joy derived from imagining future pleasures. Even though it's technically thinking about the future, we can pay attention to how we experience it in the present.

Where do you feel Vorfreude in your body?

A flutter in your stomach, ☐

a lightness in your step, ☐

shallow breaths, ☐

tingling arms... ☐

Vorfreude scale:

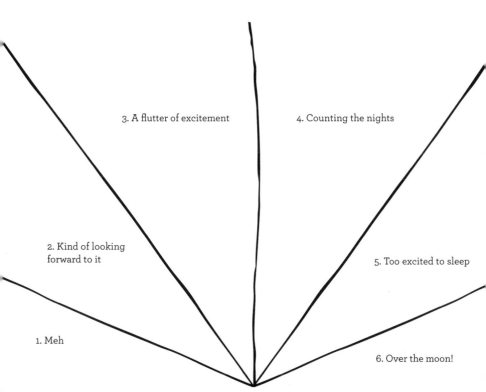

1. Meh

2. Kind of looking forward to it

3. A flutter of excitement

4. Counting the nights

5. Too excited to sleep

6. Over the moon!

Fill in the spaces below with the future plans you're looking forward to right now. Rate them using the Vorfreude scale.

Date: _14/05/2015_
Vorfreude scale: _5_

going to the

Wilderness Festival

Date: _____
Vorfreude scale: ____

Date: _____
Vorfreude scale: ____

Date: _____
Vorfreude scale: ____

Date: _13/06/2015_
Vorfreude scale: _4_

seeing my brother

this weekend

Once these are full, write new ones on Post-it notes. Stick them here and compile them high.

Outside the box

Connect all nine of these dots by making only **four straight lines** without lifting your pencil from the page and without retracing along any of the lines.

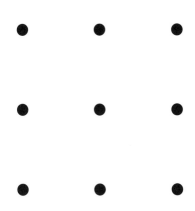

Did any of these thoughts come up?

'Oh, I know this.'

'Oh, I don't have the patience for this exercise!'

'This is so obvious.'

'I've never been good at these types of things.'

'I tried to figure this out once and totally failed.'

'I'm not going to waste my time on this.'

'I'll come back to this later.'

'I'll just take a look at the answer.'

Whatever you're thinking, just stay with this for 5 minutes if you don't already know the solution.

Then go to page 148.

Flower

Buy or pick a flower.
See it with open eyes.
Smell it with closed eyes.
Feel it with closed eyes.
Visualize it with closed eyes.
Draw it with open eyes.

Start your flower here

P.S. Now give your flower water and enjoy it until it has faded.
Then draw it again.

Emotimaps

Emotions are experienced in our bodies as well as our minds. Colour, scribble and annotate the body maps below to reflect how you experience the following emotions in your own body.

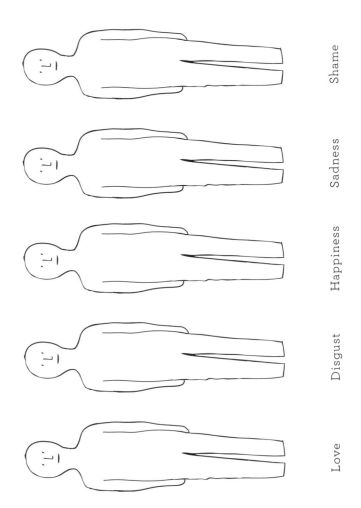

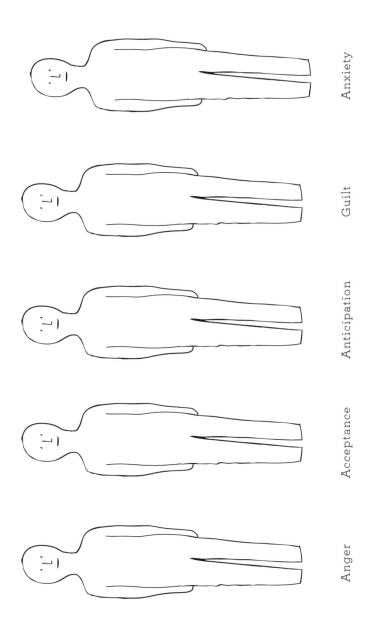

Anxiety

Guilt

Anticipation

Acceptance

Anger

Heaven or hell

'The mind is its own place, and in itself can make a heaven of hell, a hell of heaven.'

John Milton, Paradise Lost

Heaven of hell

Hellish situation:

Heavenly thoughts:

Hell of heaven

Heavenly situation:

Hellish thoughts:

Hand-washing meditation

Turn on the water and find a temperature
that is just the right warmth...

Take the soap in your hand and lather...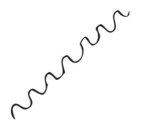

Feeling your fingers interlace and weave
back and forth in their intuitive way...

Take in the aroma of the soap before
watching the lather slowly wash away...

Dry your hands with care...

Feel the sensation of warmth and
aliveness in your fingertips.

Carry on with your day.

◊

Plant a seed

Plant a seed (or buy a small plant). Name it. Tend to it every day and watch it mindfully. Draw how it changes over time. Set a reminder to do a sketch per week.

My name is:

Week 1

Week 2

Week 3

Week 4

Week 5

Week 6

Spotted

Wear two different coloured socks today.

\ /
_OR_
/ \

Wear your shirt inside out.

Does anyone notice?

Use as needed.

Emergency exit

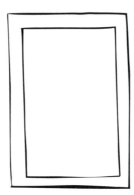

1. Stop what you're doing for a moment.
2. Take three conscious breaths.
3. Ask yourself: What is going on for me right now...in bodily sensations...in thoughts...and in feelings?
4. Notice and acknowledge your experience in this moment with a kind attention.
5. ...Keep breathing and carry on.

Tear out this page and carry it with you at all times.

A few of my favourite things

Make a list of small things that make your heart sing.

Examples:

- Walking through puddles with wellies on
- Thinking you have to get up for work and realizing it's your day off
- Giving up your seat for someone who really needs it
- The longest day of the summer
- Campfires
- Seeing a cat lying in the sun
- Spring mornings when the sun shines through new leaves and the birds are singing

1. _____
2. _____
3. _____
4. _____
5. _____
6. _____
7. _____
8. _____
9. _____
10. _____

Happy faces

Humans, pets, wild animals, buildings, cars, appliances, print, trees. Look for smiling faces everywhere and draw them here.

When you feel sad come back here and smile!

Sit...   **still**

Sit still in one place for 15 minutes.
No instructions, except: don't do anything.

100% horrid

On a scale of 1 to 100, how uncomfortable was it?

a-ok

Shocking fact:

Researchers at the University of Virginia discovered that some people would rather self-administer painful shocks than sit quietly with their own thoughts for 15 minutes.

Impermanence

Make of list of PAST worries, joys, challenges and triumphs.

Make of list of CURRENT worries, joys, challenges and triumphs.

Turn the page

Nothing is final. Just keep moving.

Reminder

Cut out and colour the following reminder. Put it in your wallet, on your desk, or by your bed. Hold it out and take pictures with it in the foreground. Share the photos of your present moments with others. #iamherenow

Most of all tune into it and practise being here now.

Am I here now?

Staying power

Instructions: put a pot of water on the hob to boil. Simply stand by without running off to do something else. Watch what bubbles up, both in the pan and in your mind and body.

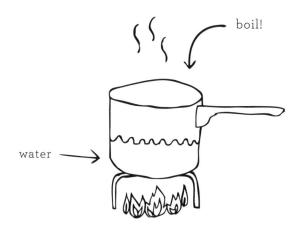

boil!

water →

Were you able to stay with it?

☐ Yes.
☐ No, I did _____ instead.

Now turn to page 117.

The time is...

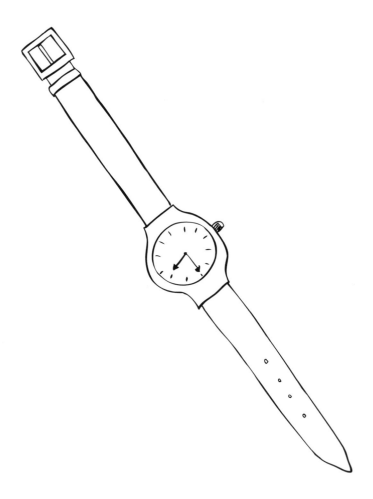

...now

1. Cut a piece of Scotch or Cellotape about 2cm x 1cm.

2. With a marker or felt tip pen write the word 'NOW' on it.

3. Allow the ink to dry.

4. Place the tape over the face of your watch face.

5. Repeat proportionally with other timepieces, at home and work.

'Forever is composed of nows.'
Emily Dickinson

Meditation map

Map key

 Park

 Meditation centre

 Museum

Toilet

Church

Beach

Mountain top

Restaurant

 Lake

Hotel / resort

River/ stream

Public transport

Forest

 Home

Walking trail

Think of all the cool places you could meditate. Use the key to make your own map of mindful places in your town or world. Tweet with #iamherenow to share your places with others.

Location(s): (not to scale)

Let go

Write on the balloons all the things you want to let go of.
Draw more balloons until the pages
are full.

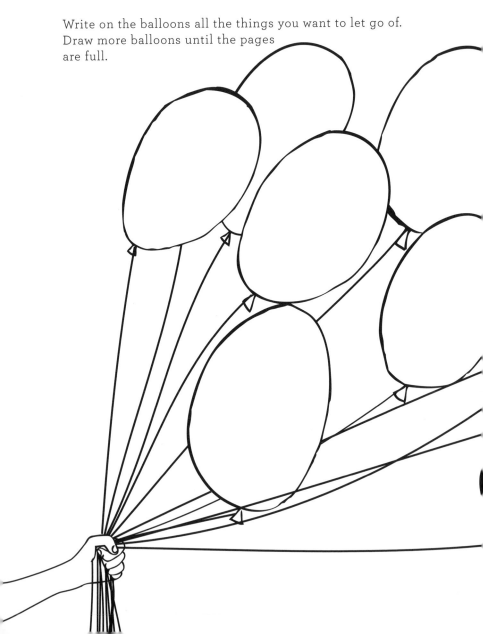

Go outside, close your eyes and let them sail off
into the sky.

Scentsation

'Memories, imagination, old sentiments,
and associations are more readily reached
through the sense of smell than through any
other channel.'

Oliver Wendell Holmes

Capture a scent if you can – dab a drop of perfume or laundry detergent...or glue a sprinkle of dirt or cinnamon on the page.

Deposit scent here

How does the scent make you feel?

It's a zoo in here!

If your mind were an animal today, what would it be...

A monkey, wildly swinging from tree to tree?
A giraffe, peacefully surveying the scene?
A penguin, cheerfully hanging out in the cold?
A camel, slowly making its way through the day?
An ostrich, hightailing it around?
An alligator on edge?
A tiger, prowling around for trouble?

Who else is in your zoo?

Digital

In what situations do you commonly find yourself checking your mobile phone? (Circle all that apply.)

Before getting out of bed

On public transport

While waiting for something or someone

During meals

On the toilet

During work

In bed

While talking to someone

In the park

On the beach

Other:

_____

Other:

_____

detox

Spend a day without your phone.

Plan your day...map your way:

Urges to check phone:

✓

Messages to send later:

Nice things noticed:

Stand still

Stand still for five minutes.

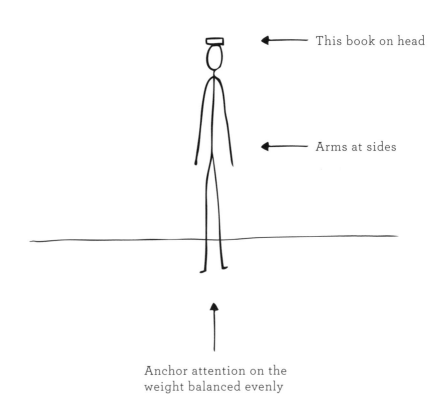

This book on head

Arms at sides

Anchor attention on the
weight balanced evenly
on feet

Mindful photography

Cut out the centre of the frame along the dotted line. Then follow the instructions on the next page.

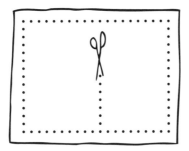

Take the book to the park (or somewhere outdoors).
Use the camera lens to capture your favourite scenes and
safely store them in your memory.

Your favourite quote

Your favourite quote:

Wheel of what ifs

Make your own wheel of worries and wonders using your mind's most common themes.

Colour in and decorate the tabs as desired.

To play, anchor a paper clip in the centre with a pencil or pen, and flick to spin!

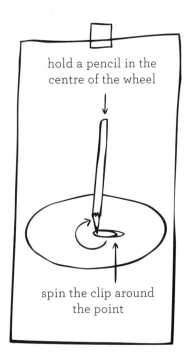

hold a pencil in the centre of the wheel

spin the clip around the point

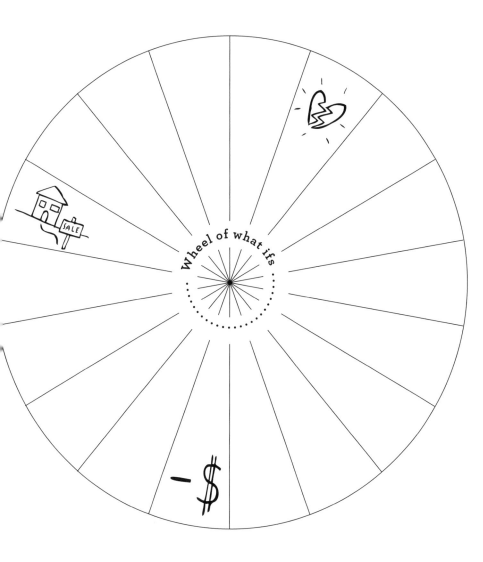

Fine print: Prizes are not guaranteed. Neither are losses.

Supply chain of wonder

Consider all the people, care, collaboration and energy that went into creating one of your favourite treats. Make a supply chain including all the steps it took to get to you.

planted

grown

harvested

packaged

manufactured

distributed

displayed

devoured

bought

Item you love: _____

Supply chain:

Really hungry

How do you know when you're hungry? What are the physical signs?

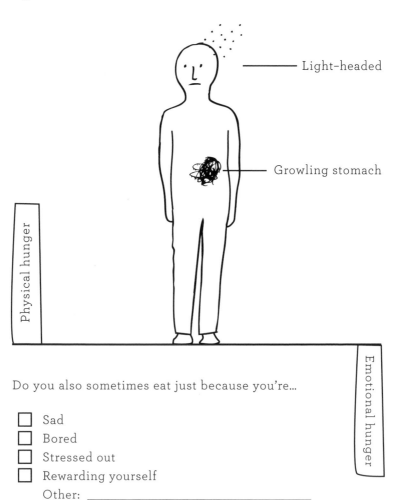

Light-headed

Growling stomach

Physical hunger

Emotional hunger

Do you also sometimes eat just because you're...

☐ Sad
☐ Bored
☐ Stressed out
☐ Rewarding yourself
   Other: _____

Next time you're about to eat, tune into your levels of physical and emotional hunger. Make a dot where the levels connect on the following chart. Continue plotting observations over time and notice any patterns.

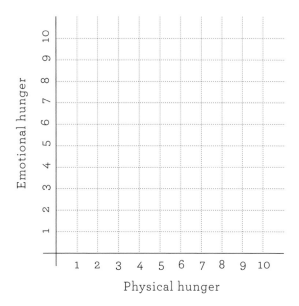

Notes:
_____

_____

_____

_____

Footnote:

There's no right or wrong here. Mindfulness is about cultivating non-judgemental awareness of our experiences and patterns. Just be curious!

Breathing and weaving

Pick two colours. With your eyes closed, imagine breathing in one colour and out the other. Repeat with different colours and weave them all together here.

out breath colour ⟶

in breath colour ↑

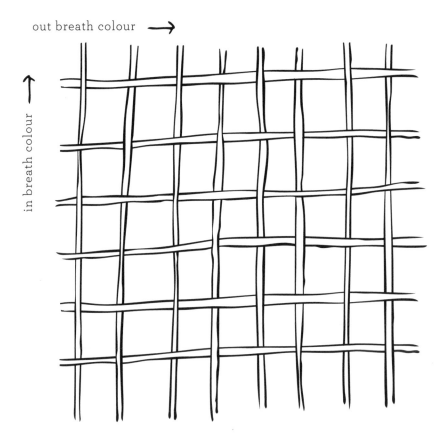

Habit breaker

Cut out the habit breakers on the corners of this page and, with a piece of tape, stick them somewhere to remind you of a habit you'd like to break. Examples: phone-checking, coffee-drinking, refrigerator-ravaging, TV-watching, computer-surfing/gaming etc.

Make a tick here every time you wanted to _____ or _____ but didn't, thanks to the sticker.

The ~~to do~~ list

Write down a list of things you're planning to do today...

_____

_____

_____

_____

_____

_____

_____

_____

_____

_____

_____

_____

_____

_____

_____

Now DON'T do them.

The ~~to do~~ list

Write down a list of things that you've been dreading or putting off...

_____

_____

_____

_____

_____

_____

_____

_____

_____

_____

_____

_____

_____

_____

_____

_____

_____

_____

_____

Now DO do them.

Vital signs – heart beat

1. Set the timer for one minute.
2. Put two right-hand fingers on the pulse point of your neck.
3. Draw a line for each pulse you feel, with your eyes closed.

Repeat this exercise, using a different coloured pen each time.

- Don't worry if you miss any.
- When your mind wanders off, just gently bring your attention back to sensation of the pulse.

Random leaf I found...

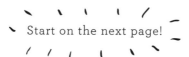

Start on the next page!

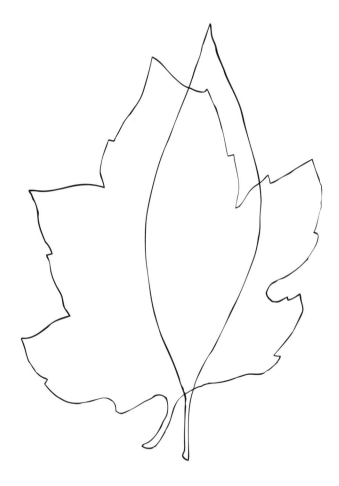

1. Place your leaf here.
2. Staple this and the previous page together where marked.

More instructions on next page!

...and now appreciate

1. Trace the leaf between the pages with your finger.

2. Use a crayon or coloured pencil to rub over the leaf.

3. Look at the shape and all the little veins that are revealed.

4. Notice the smell of the leaf.

5. Turn back to page 113 and repeat.

Hi tea!

Make yourself a cup of your favourite tea.

Smell the aroma

Taste the flavour

Feel the temperature

Enjoy it mindfully.

Decorate the mug when you've finished.

Sleep aid

Practise meditation lying down

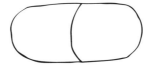

Your mind is racing as you are trying to sleep.
Trying so hard that you are wide-awake.
So many thoughts as time passes by.
Tomorrow's day will be a tired one.

Surrender to your thoughts.
Let them come and go like clouds.
Breathe them in and breathe them out.
This breath, this breath and this breath.

The one who falls asleep is not trying.
Falling asleep when tiredness comes.
Letting wakefulness be.
Not trying, just accepting.

Place one hand on your belly and one on your heart.
Let kindness float into your body.
Let the thoughts come and go like sheep.
Let sleep be.

Trophy case

On this page, give yourself credit for things you've achieved, accomplished, and done well. Large and small, colour in the trophies and label them with your actions of simple awesomeness!

Breathe the wave

Our breath is like a wave. It goes up as you breathe in, and down as you breathe out. Grab a pen and draw waves with your breath.

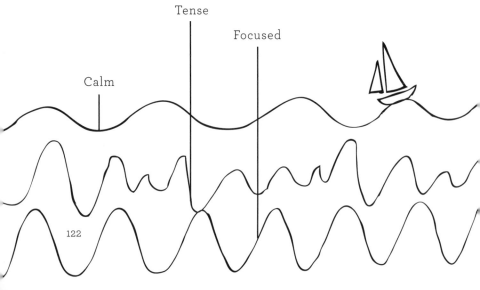

Calm

Tense

Focused

Hints:

The in-breath energizes the body, the out breath relaxes it.

The in-breath activates the sympathetic nervous system, the out breath the parasympathetic nervous system.

When you are feeling tired and dull during meditation, focus on your in-breath. When you are feeling anxious/agitated, focus on your out-breath.

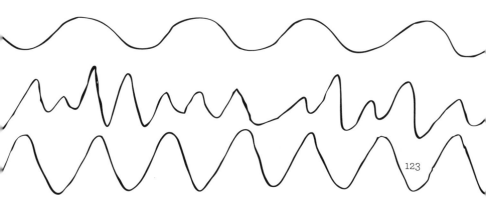

Escape-aid

Sometimes when the present moment gets uncomfortable, we feel the urge to distract ourselves or escape from the here and now. An escape-aid could be aimlessly checking social media or grabbing another cup of coffee.

Note the things you do to help you escape or give you a quick fix.

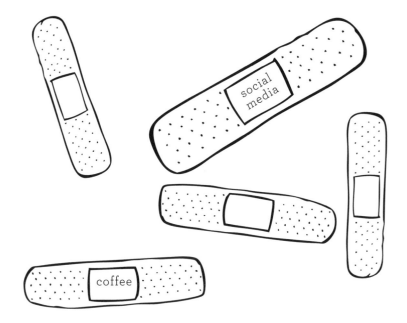

Practise surfing the urges...

Urge surfing

Feel the urge start to arise.

Notice how it feels in the body and stay with the sensations.

Ride out the urge without giving in to it.

'Between stimulus and response there is a space. In that space lies our freedom and power to choose our response'

Unknown, from Stephen Covey

One less regret

Think of a close friend that you've lost contact with over the years.

Write them a letter,

find a way to get their address,

and send it off.

Dear _____

Warts and all

Draw a face that represents a good friend or loved one here. Then write all the things you like about them and all their weaknesses. Be honest.

Love them anyway

'True love isn't about finding the perfect person to love, but rather learning to love and accept someone despite all their imperfections.'

Unknown

Star gazing

Pay attention to the night sky and check these off as you see them.

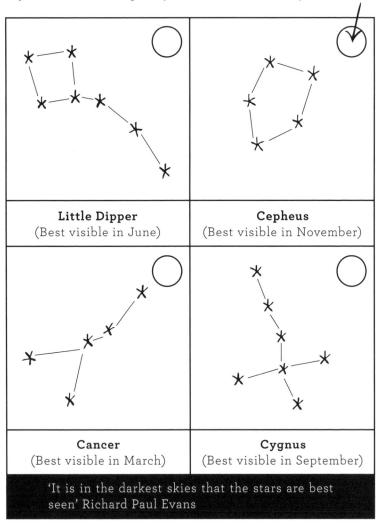

Little Dipper (Best visible in June)	**Cepheus** (Best visible in November)
Cancer (Best visible in March)	**Cygnus** (Best visible in September)

'It is in the darkest skies that the stars are best seen' Richard Paul Evans

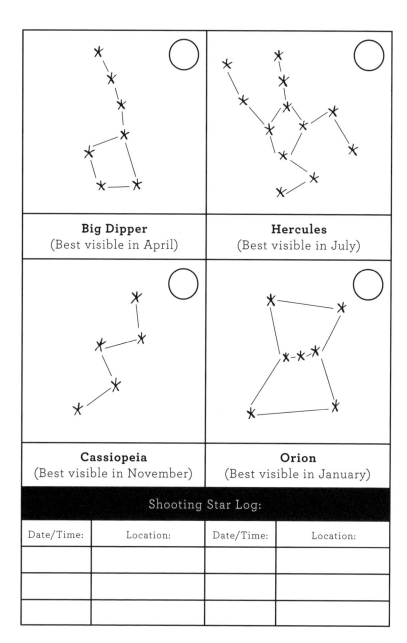

Big Dipper
(Best visible in April)

Hercules
(Best visible in July)

Cassiopeia
(Best visible in November)

Orion
(Best visible in January)

Shooting Star Log:

Date/Time:	Location:	Date/Time:	Location:

Un-hook

When you're meditating and your mind drifts off into thinking, make a *mental note* of where it went to, un-hook it and come back to your breath.

Hooks to look out for:

- Thinking about the past
- Worrying
- Day dreaming
- Planning
- Analysing
- Judging

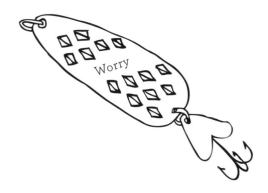

Note the topics that came up on the
hooks and add more as necessary.

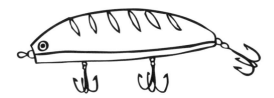

Pet rock

Find an average-looking rock and let it become your companion. Carry it around in your pocket for a week and make a space for it on your bedside table.

Pay unconditional attention to it while you:

- Pick it up
- Rinse it off
- Name it
- Decorate it
- Show it to your friends
- Sketch it

Notice how your relationship with the rock changes over the week.

Rock's name: _____

Portrait:

Activity log:
(e.g. sunsets, dinners, TV shows, walks)

_____

_____

_____

_____

_____

_____

Playing attention

Rip out the next page – make an aeroplane and throw it out the window. Pay close attention as it flies down.

INSTRUCTIONS:

1. Fold the paper in half lengthways.
2. Open the paper up again.
3. Fold the top corners in to meet the centre fold line.
4. Fold the sides in again to meet the centre (along the dotted lines).
5. Fold the whole thing together.
6. Fold each outer side in half again.
7. Fly it.

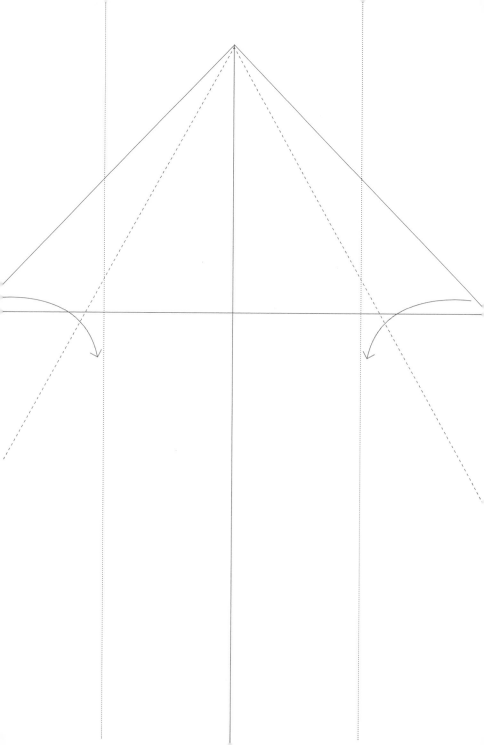

Extra credit: Write a poem on the page before making the plane.

Watch as someone picks it up and reads it OR decorate the aeroplane and give it to someone else to play with when you've finished.

Blank page, just for fun.

The itch

Meditate for 7.5 minutes. Watch out for an itch to appear.
Notice it, welcome it to your experience.

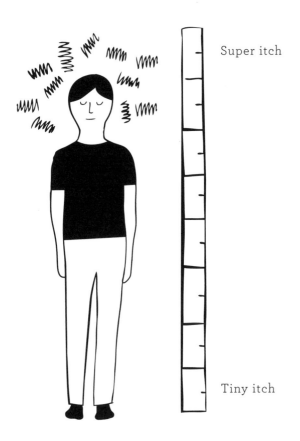

Super itch

Tiny itch

Be with it, as long as you can. Repeat as necessary.

Tear out the page

Watch a sad film.

Set your sadness free and collect your tears on the page.

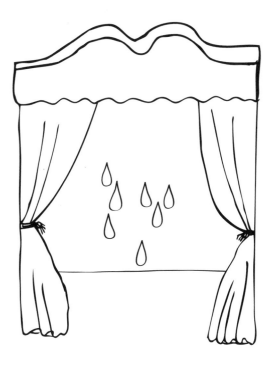

Then bring yourself back and direct your attention to the next exercise...

Song love

Turn on a song you love.

Listen.

Notice how the sounds and lyrics resonate in your body.

Sing

Dance

Repeat

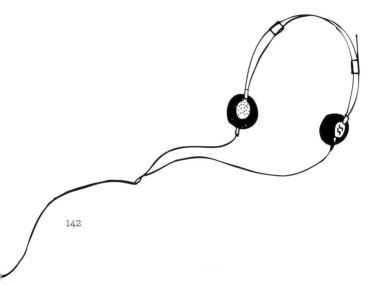

Note your favourite lyrics here:

Up the wall

Plaster these walls with all the things that drive you crazy...
self-criticisms, pet peeves, worries, negative thoughts.

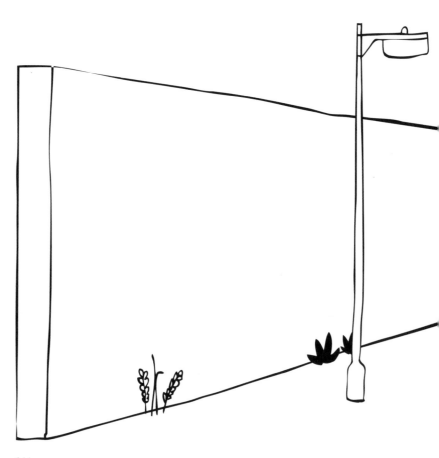

Overlapping, in every direction. In all colours, shapes and sizes.

Make these your graffiti walls.

Gratitude alarm

Set an alarm for every 60 minutes. Use it as a reminder to be grateful. Document your findings here.

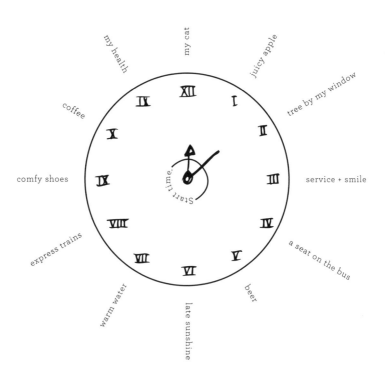

Outside the box

From page 62.

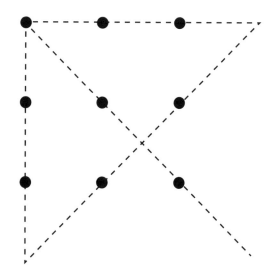

Did you find yourself limiting the possible solutions by the form of the box that was already there?

This exercise is actually from where the phrase 'think outside the box' originates.

Coffee contest

Try different coffee shops in your neighbourhood. Rank the coffees according to their flavour. Give the winner a thank you note.

Name:	Name:
Taste: _____ _____ _____ Rank: _____	Taste: _____ _____ _____ Rank: _____
Name: Taste: _____ _____ _____ Rank: _____	Dear: _____ You make the best coffee around. Thanks for being here.

Give thanks.

Thanks!

Best wishes

Attach a picture of yourself as a child here:

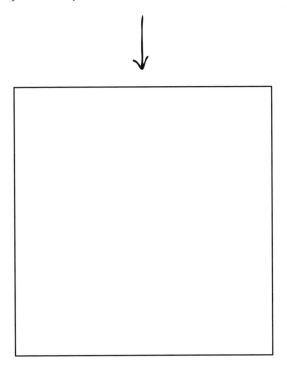

Aww, just look at you!

Remember this lovely, innocent and vulnerable child in you and make a wish for yourself to be truly happy, healthy and at peace.

Chewing gum meditation

Instructions:

Take a piece of chewing gum and place it on the palm of your hand.

Look at it as if you've never seen a piece of gum before.

Break it in half and smell it. Notice if your mouth is watering.

Slowly place it on your tongue and start chewing.

Notice the intensity of the flavour as you take the first few chews and see if it changes over time.

Carry on chewing as you normally would.

Practise with different brands and flavours of chewing gum.
Make notes here. Use a different coloured pen for each one.

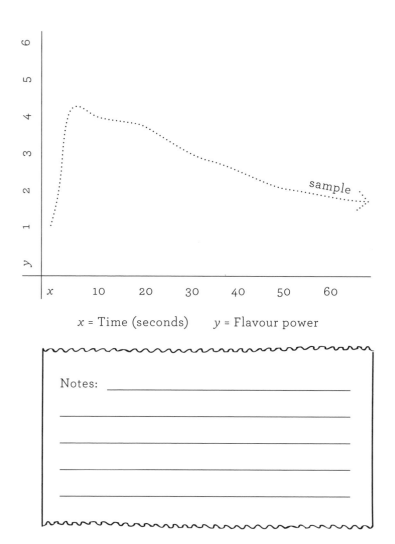

x = Time (seconds) y = Flavour power

Notes: _____

_____

_____

_____

_____

Push my buttons

What are your top three hot buttons?
Who or what tends to push them?

1. _____

2. _____

3. _____

How do you usually react?
Try taking 3 mindful breaths next time and see what happens.

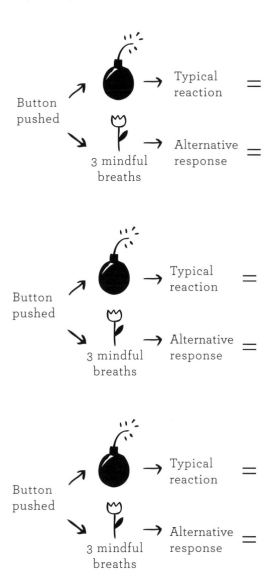

Aimless wandering

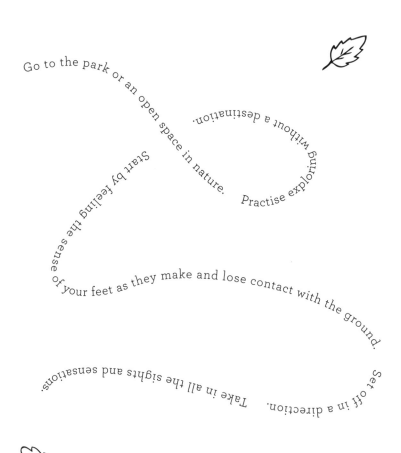

Go to the park or an open space in nature. Start by feeling the sense of your feet as they make and lose contact with the ground. Practise exploring without a destination. Set off in a direction. Take in all the sights and sensations.

P.S. When your thoughts wander off in a different direction, just bring your attention back to your feet.

'As you start to walk out on the way,
the way appears.'

Rumi

Hang loose

Sometimes you've just got to *hang loose*.

Pick your favourite relaxing activity and do it.
Here are some ideas – add your own and check them off as
you do them:

☐ Lying in a hammock.
☐ Rolling down a grassy hill.
☐ Floating on your back in the pool.
☐ Sitting on a bench in the sun.
☐ Listening to a cat purr.
☐ _____
☐ _____
☐ _____
☐ _____
☐ _____
☐ _____
☐ _____
☐ _____
☐ _____
☐ _____

Meditation hurdles

Meditating can, at times, be like running on a track with hurdles. Our minds and bodies encounter all kinds of hindrances to meditating before, during and after practice.

Some examples:

'It's too hard'

'It won't work for me'

'I don't have the time'

'I'd rather do something else'

Busy mind

'It's boring'

'I'm not good at this'

Restlessness

Sleepiness

Label the hurdles with your top 5.

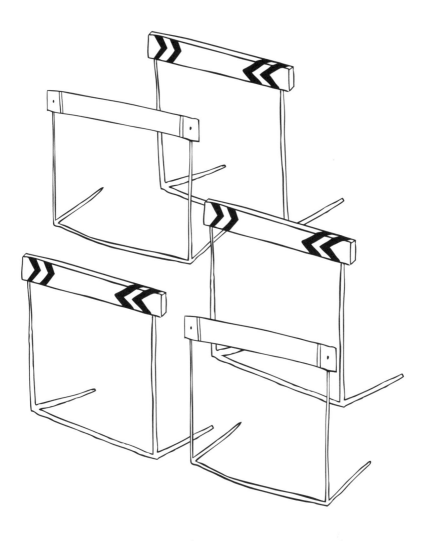

Extra credit: watch a YouTube video of runners to see how they deal with the hurdles.

Group hug

Draw all of your closest people here – if you can't think of anyone just include the people you see on a daily basis.

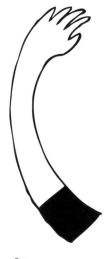

Close your eyes and think of all the warm-heartedness, love and kindness they have for you.

And bring to mind all of the goodwill you hold for them. Notice how it feels in your body to hold all of these people in your heart.

Mindfulness game

To play, anchor a paper clip in the centre of the dice with a pencil/pen, and flick to spin!

Hang loose
page 158

look into
your friend's
eyes for 30
seconds

Song love
page 142

meditate for
5 mins

Vit

start over
(with ease)

Staying
power
page 85

page 75

take 3 deep
breaths

start

pause and
spin again

Emergency
exit

meditate for
3 mins

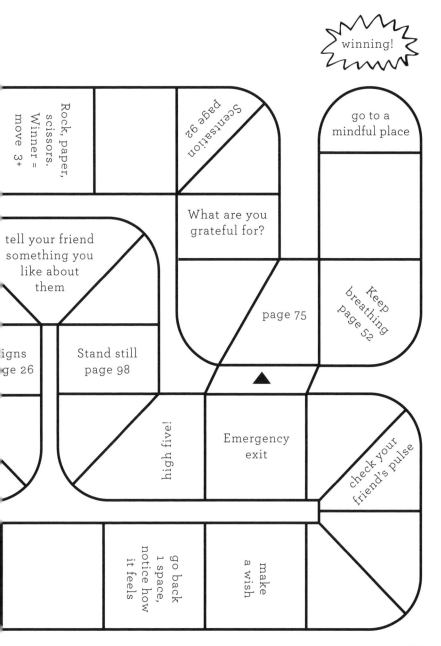

winning!

Rock, paper, scissors. Winner = move 3+

Scentsation page 92

go to a mindful place

What are you grateful for?

tell your friend something you like about them

page 75

Keep breathing page 52

igns ge 26

Stand still page 98

high five!

Emergency exit

check your friend's pulse

go back 1 space, notice how it feels

make a wish

Meditation field notes

Follow the guided audio practice(s) outlined on page 18 and available at:

www.iamherenow.com

The field notes pages that follow are designed for you to record notes from your formal meditation practice. Photocopy these blank pages so you always have spares at hand.

Also, on the following page, you'll find tips on how to sit to further help you with your meditation practice.

⟶ P.S. The same Frames of mindfulness (page 12) and ways for How to be here now (page 16) introduced in the beginning of the book apply to meditation practice.

Tips on how to sit

There are several ways you can sit when meditating. Find one that is comfortable for you. Try the following and select your favourite.

☐ **On a chair**

Sit on a chair with your feet planted on the floor or on a block/book if they don't reach the floor. Your thighs should be horizontal. Try sitting away from the back of the chair if possible.

☐ **On your knees**

Straddle a cushion, bolster or block in a kneeling position on a mat or rug. Rest your hands on a pillow or cushion in your lap if that's comfortable.

☐ **Cross-legged**

Sit on a flat surface with your legs crossed in a way that's comfortable. You may want to sit with a cushion underneath you, so your knees are pointed downward and supported by the ground. Or you can sit flat on the ground and put a support under each knee. Settle your upper body into an upright and alert posture.

Keep the spine straight and aligned with the head and neck. Relax the shoulders by taking a deep breath in and releasing with the out breath. Lift your hands up and let them fall naturally to a comfortable position on your thighs or fold them in your lap. Gently close your eyes.

Field notes (example)

Date: __APRIL 27__ Time: __10·15__ Practice length: __10 MINS__

Posture: (Lying) | Sitting | Standing

Location: __LIVING ROOM (IN SUNNY CORNER)__

Mood (circle one):   Words: Body map:

Before: __TIRED__

After: 😊 😐 ☹   __REFRESHED__

Notes (Thoughts / Senses / Emotions):

FELT TIRED AT FIRST. HAD THOUGHTS / WORRIES ABOUT MY PRESENTATION, BUT WAS ABLE TO COME BACK TO MY BREATH. NOTICED THAT WHEN I HAD THE WORRIES, MY SHOULDER STARTED TENSING AND MY STOMACH WAS A BIT NERVOUS.

REALLY FELT MY BREATH IN MY WHOLE TORSO BY THE END ALSO NOTICED MY PULSE IN MY FINGERTIPS.

Other:

GRATEFUL FOR SUNSHINE TODAY!

LOOKING FORWARD TO MY TRIP THIS WEEKEND.

SEND BIRTHDAY CARD TO MUM

Field notes

Date: _____ Time: _____ Practice length: _____

Posture: | Lying | Sitting | Standing

Location: _____

Mood (circle one):   Words: Body map:

Before: ☺   😐   ☹   _____

After: ☺   😐   ☹   _____

Notes (Thoughts / Senses / Emotions):

_____

_____

_____

_____

_____

_____

_____

_____

_____

_____

Other:

Field notes

Date: _____ Time: _____ Practice length: _____

Posture: | Lying | Sitting | Standing

Location: _____

Mood (circle one):   Words: Body map:

Before: ☺ 😐 ☹ _____

After: ☺ 😐 ☹ _____

Notes (Thoughts / Senses / Emotions):

_____

_____

_____

_____

_____

_____

_____

_____

_____

_____

Other:

Field notes

Date: _____ Time: _____ Practice length: _____

Posture: | Lying | Sitting | Standing

Location: _____

Mood (circle one):   Words: Body map:

Before: ☺ 😐 ☹ _____

After: ☺ 😐 ☹ _____

Notes (Thoughts / Senses / Emotions):

_____

_____

_____

_____

_____

_____

_____

_____

_____

_____

Other:

Field notes

Date: _____ Time: _____ Practice length: _____

Posture: | Lying | Sitting | Standing

Location: _____

Mood (circle one):   Words: Body map:

Before: ☺ ☻ ☹ _____

After: ☺ ☻ ☹ _____

Notes (Thoughts / Senses / Emotions):

_____

_____

_____

_____

_____

_____

_____

_____

_____

_____

Other:

Field notes

Date: _____ Time: _____ Practice length: _____

Posture: | Lying | Sitting | Standing

Location: _____

Mood (circle one):   Words: Body map:

Before: ☺ 😐 ☹ _____

After: ☺ 😐 ☹ _____

Notes (Thoughts / Senses / Emotions):

_____

_____

_____

_____

_____

_____

_____

_____

_____

_____

Other:

Field notes

Date: _____ Time: _____ Practice length: _____

Posture: | Lying | Sitting | Standing

Location: _____

Mood (circle one):   Words: Body map:

Before: :) :| :(_____

After: :) :| :(_____

Notes (Thoughts / Senses / Emotions):

_____

_____

_____

_____

_____

_____

_____

_____

_____

_____

Other:

Field notes

Date: _____ Time: _____ Practice length: _____

Posture: | Lying | Sitting | Standing

Location: _____

Mood (circle one):   Words: Body map:

Before: ☺ 😐 ☹ _____

After: ☺ 😐 ☹ _____

Notes (Thoughts / Senses / Emotions):

_____

_____

_____

_____

_____

_____

_____

_____

_____

_____

Other:

Field notes

Date: _____ Time: _____ Practice length: _____

Posture: | Lying | Sitting | Standing

Location: _____

Mood (circle one):   Words: Body map:

Before: ☺ ☺ ☹ _____

After: ☺ ☺ ☹ _____

Notes (Thoughts / Senses / Emotions):

_____

_____

_____

_____

_____

_____

_____

_____

_____

_____

Other:

Field notes

Date: _____ Time: _____ Practice length: _____

Posture: | Lying | Sitting | Standing

Location: _____

Mood (circle one):   Words: Body map:

Before: ☺ 😐 ☹   _____

After: ☺ 😐 ☹   _____

Notes (Thoughts / Senses / Emotions):

_____

_____

_____

_____

_____

_____

_____

_____

_____

_____

Other:

Field notes

Date: _____ Time: _____ Practice length: _____

Posture: | Lying | Sitting | Standing

Location: _____

Mood (circle one):   Words: Body map:

Before: ☺ ☺ ☹   _____

After: ☺ ☺ ☹   _____

Notes (Thoughts / Senses / Emotions):

_____

_____

_____

_____

_____

_____

_____

_____

_____

_____

Other:

Field notes

Date: _____ Time: _____ Practice length: _____

Posture: | Lying | Sitting | Standing

Location: _____

Mood (circle one):   Words: Body map:

Before: ☺   ☹   ☹   _____

After: ☺   ☹   ☹   _____

Notes (Thoughts / Senses / Emotions):

_____

_____

_____

_____

_____

_____

_____

_____

_____

_____

Other:

Field notes

Date: _____ Time: _____ Practice length: _____

Posture: | Lying | Sitting | Standing

Location: _____

Mood (circle one):   Words: Body map:

Before: ☺ ☺ ☹ _____

After: ☺ ☺ ☹ _____

Notes (Thoughts / Senses / Emotions):

_____

_____

_____

_____

_____

_____

_____

_____

_____

_____

Other:

Field notes

Date: _____ Time: _____ Practice length: _____

Posture: | Lying | Sitting | Standing

Location: _____

Mood (circle one):   Words: Body map:

Before: ☺ ☹ ☹ _____

After: ☺ ☹ ☹ _____

Notes (Thoughts / Senses / Emotions):

_____

_____

_____

_____

_____

_____

_____

_____

_____

_____

Other:

Field notes

Date: _____ Time: _____ Practice length: _____

Posture: | Lying | Sitting | Standing

Location: _____

Mood (circle one):   Words: Body map:

Before: ☺ ☺ ☹ _____

After: ☺ ☺ ☹ _____

Notes (Thoughts / Senses / Emotions):

_____

_____

_____

_____

_____

_____

_____

_____

_____

_____

Other:

The authors of this book, Alexandra Frey and Autumn Totton, are the founders
of The Mindfulness Project.

The Mindfulness Project is a platform for teaching and spreading mindfulness,
which is done through a centre in London and internationally through a range
of online programmes. Its team of expert teachers runs 8-week courses to
build the essential skills of mindfulness and also offers advanced courses,
drop-in classes, workshops and seminars on a range of mindful-living topics.
Alexandra, Autumn and everyone at The Mindfulness Project are deeply
motivated by the way the practice has changed and enriched their own lives
and by the huge evidence base that shows it has the potential to do the same
for many others. Learn more at: www.londonmindful.com

10 9 8
Ebury Press, an imprint of Ebury Publishing,
20 Vauxhall Bridge Road,
London, SW1V 2SA

Penguin
Random House
UK

Ebury Press is part of the Penguin Random House group of companies whose
addresses can be found at global.penguinrandomhouse.com

First published by Ebury Press in 2015 (www.eburypublishing.co.uk)

A CIP catalogue record for this book is available from the British Library
ISBN: 9781785030772

Designed by Pirrip Press
Printed and bound in Slovakia by TBB, a.s.

Penguin Random House is committed to a sustainable future for
our business, our readers and our planet. This book is made from
Forest Stewardship Council® certified paper.